Maple Syrup

PURE MAPLE SYRUP

Helen Lepp Friesen

Weigl

Published by Weigl Educational Publishers Limited
6325 10th Street SE
Calgary, Alberta T2H 2Z9
Website: www.weigl.ca

Library and Archives Canada Cataloguing in Publication

Friesen, Helen Lepp, 1961-
        Maple syrup / Helen Lepp Friesen.

(Canadian icons)
Includes index.
ISBN 978-1-77071-660-5 (bound).--ISBN 978-1-77071-666-7 (pbk.)
        1. Maple syrup--Canada--Juvenile literature.
I. Title. II. Series: Canadian icons

TP395.F75 2011   j641.3'364   C2011-900805-X

Printed in the United States of America in North Mankato, Minnesota
1 2 3 4 5 6 7 8 9 0 15 14 13 12 11

052011
WEP37500

Editor: Heather Kissock
Design: Terry Paulhus

Weigl acknowledges Getty Images as the primary image supplier for this title.

We acknowledge the financial support of the Government of Canada through the Canada Book Fund for our
publishing activities.

CONTENTS

What is Maple Syrup?

Canada is known for its maple trees. Every year, **sap** flows from these trees. People collect the sap and make maple syrup with it. Maple syrup is a thick, sticky **liquid**. It is used to make foods taste sweet.

4

6

A Sappy Past

Long before Europeans came to Canada, **First Nations** peoples used the sap from maple trees to sweeten food. To get the sap, they put holes in the tree. They then hung birchbark baskets under the hole. The baskets were used to catch the sap.

When Europeans arrived in the area, First Nations peoples showed them how to get sap from the trees. The Europeans called this tapping the tree.

The Sugar Maple

Most maple syrup comes from a tree called the sugar maple. In Canada, most sugar maples are found in the **Maritimes**, Quebec, and Ontario. Sugar maples are tall trees. They can grow up to 35 metres high. Their leaves have five points.

Sugaring Off

Over the winter months, a maple tree's sap stays inside the tree. When spring arrives, the weather turns warm. The sap begins to run from the trees. This is called sugaring off. The sap runs for three to six weeks. People tap the trees and gather the sap at this time.

10

Tapping the Trees

To tap a tree, people drill a small hole into it. The hole is drilled about 1 metre from the ground. A **spile** is then hammered into the hole. The sap runs from the spile and into a bucket. Up to 40 litres of sap can come from one tap hole.

The Sugar Hut

The sap is removed from the buckets every day. It is poured through a **filter**. This removes twigs, bark, and dirt that may have fallen into the bucket. The sap is then stored in big barrels.

When enough sap is collected, it is taken to the sugar hut. Here, it is boiled in a big kettle or pan to make syrup.

Boiling the Sap

The sap is boiled to remove water from it. The water is removed through **evaporation**. This turns the water into steam. The steam rises from the sap and drifts away.

It takes a long time to boil off the water. When all of the water is gone, only the maple syrup remains.

Tasty Syrup

Canada's maple syrup is sold all over the world. People use it in many ways. Some people pour it on their pancakes. Others bake treats with it. Maple syrup can also be used to make candy.

More Maple

The sap from maple trees makes more than syrup. If the sap boils long enough, it turns into taffy. Taffy is a thick, chewy candy.

Maple butter is also made by boiling sap. Maple butter can be spread on bread like jam. It can also be used as icing on a cake.

Maple sugar is made when the sap is boiled for a very long time. It can be used in place of white sugar.

Snow Taffy

Supplies

3/4 cup water

2 cups
brown sugar

1 1/4 cups
corn syrup

2 tablespoons
butter

snow

vanilla

1 teaspoon salt

popsicle sticks

wooden spoon

pot

1. Mix brown sugar, corn syrup, water, and salt in a pot. Stir with a wooden spoon.

2. With an adult's help, place the mixture on low heat. Stir until the sugar has dissolved.

3. Increase the heat, and boil the mixture for five minutes.

4. Add butter. Stir slowly.

5. Add vanilla.

6. Pour the mixture in strips 10 centimetres long onto the snow.

7. Roll the taffy onto popsicle sticks.

8. Enjoy.

Find Out More

To find out more about maple syrup, visit these websites.

A History of Maple Syrup
www.canadianmaplesyrup.com/
maplehistory.html

Maple Syrup Festivals in Canada
http://gocanada.about.com/od/
canadawithkids/ss/maple_syrup.htm

Settling Canada—Syrup
www.histori.ca/minutes/
minute.do?id=10128

Glossary

evaporation: when a liquid turns into a gas

filter: a material with tiny spaces in it that catches dirt or other matter

First Nations: the first people to live in what is now Canada

liquid: matter that is not a solid or a gas

Maritimes: the provinces along the east coast of Canada, including New Brunswick, Nova Scotia, and Prince Edward Island

sap: a liquid that flows through a plant

spile: a wooden spout

Index